MORGAN ROSE was born in New Orleans, grew up in New Mexico, and currently lives in Melbourne. She is an internationally produced playwright and performance maker. Her work is contemporary and darkly funny, with an element of absurdism. In addition to her text-based work she has a background in physical theatre and devising. She has studied with SITI Company (NYC, USA), Pacific Performance Project (Seattle, USA), Zen Zen Zo Physical Theatre (Brisbane, Australia), and Dairakudakan (Hakuba, Japan). She completed a Master of Writing for Performance at VCA in 2013. In 2020 she was a dramaturgy placement with Malthouse Theatre as part of the Besen Family Artist Program. She was a recipient of the INK writing commission with Red Stitch Actors Theatre in 2014 and again in 2018. Recent works include: *Virgins and Cowboys* (writer, Theatreworks, Griffin Theatre), *F.* (writer, Riot Stage/ Poppyseed Festival), *Lord Willing and the Creek Don't Rise* (writer, MKA/MTC NEON), *The BachelorS17E05* (co-creator, La Mama), and *desert, 6:29pm* (writer, Red Stitch/Wuzhen Festival). She is currently the resident writer at Riot Stage Youth Theatre (riotstage. com) and a co-founder of the dramaturgy initiative Lonely Company (lonelycompany.com). She is left handed.

desert, 6:29pm
Morgan Rose

CURRENCY PRESS
The performing arts publisher

CURRENCY PLAYS

First published in 2017
by Currency Press Pty Ltd,
PO Box 2287, Strawberry Hills, NSW, 2012, Australia
enquiries@currency.com.au
www.currency.com.au

This revised edition first published in 2020.

Cataloguing-in-publication data for this title is available from the National
Library of Australia website: www.nla.gov.au

Typeset by Dean Nottle for Currency Press.
Front cover image shows Eva Seymour as Xan.
Back cover image shows Ella Caldwell as Abby, Darcy Kent as Jamie, Sarah
Sutherland as Crystal, Joe Petruzzi as Rico and Eva Seymour as Xan.
Cover photography by Robert Blackburn Photography and Work Art Life Studios.
Cover layout by Emma Rose Smith for Currency Press.

Contents

Currency Press acknowledges the Traditional Owners of the Country on which we live and work. We pay our respects to all Aboriginal and Torres Strait Islander Elders, past and present.

A note on the text

In her early notes for *desert, 6:29pm* Morgan Rose referenced the haunting Bobbie Gentry song 'Ode to Billie Joe'. Recorded in 1967, this was a number one hit in the US and around the world. Its gentle, insistent acoustic guitar riff coupled with some gliding strings and Gentry's smoky, whispering tone takes you straight to the Deep South: the heartland of country music.

The song starts with brother and sister farmers heading back for lunch in the middle of a working day. You hear some phrases – *choppin' cotton, balin' hay, black-eyed peas, apple pie* – and it seems as if Gentry is conjuring a typical meal in the life of a rural, working family. And then it hits you, the phrase that finishes every verse (and there's no chorus) – *Billie Joe jumped off the Tallahatchie Bridge.*

This tension between the routine of life, the casual rhythm of family, the assumption of 'normality' and the sudden, rearing possibility of catastrophe is the springing-off point for *desert, 6:29pm.*

We are not in the Deep South, but a small country town somewhere in Australia, and Gentry's 1960s farmers are here transfigured into a contemporary working-class family. Their routine is tied not to the rhythm of sowing and reaping, but rather to the slog of service industry jobs and the low-level hum of 21st-century boredom.

The central character of *desert* is Xan, a young, gay, closeted woman on the brink of adulthood, caught in the liminal space between completing high school and the rest of her life: that last, strange summer that seems attached to both the rhythm of the past and the expectation of the future.

XAN: I could go to uni.
CRYSTAL: Well. Yeah. That's true. [*Pause*] Did you apply?
XAN: I'll probably apply next year.

This desultory, heart-breaking (and often hilarious) dialogue is the pulsing heart of Morgan's text. In its perfect form the family is a crucible of unconditional love, but in practice, of course, we stumble through:

holding each other up, loving, fighting, challenging and forgiving. It takes a particular kind of courage to break from the 'norm' in a unit as intrinsically structured as a genetic family is, and that is what is required of any queer kid who wants or needs to be heard. It's over a century since Wilde coined his immortal phrase 'the love that dares not speak its name' and we have come a heck of a long way since, but that first step is always going to be a challenge.

And this is what is at the heart of Morgan's beautiful play. It isn't about raging homophobia, but the casual assumption of heterosexuality and the consequent fear of being 'other', of feeling 'less than' which so many young queer people experience. The family at the heart of *desert, 6:29pm* are all, in their own quiet ways, struggling with despair – the fear of ageing, boredom and failure take equal place with Xan's secret life, but it is the lack of permission Xan feels to express herself which forms the engine of the story.

Despite the darkness described above, *desert* is an intensely funny, warm, quirky and ultimately optimistic play. Its crackling dialogue and wry observation of the foibles of family life are at times hilarious. And it has that incredibly satisfying quality where you feel like you are laughing out of one eye and crying out of the other. At its core, there is suicide and depression, but its beating heart is the will to survive, to face the darkness and come out, breathing at least, on the other side. Shaken, perhaps bruised, but ready to take on another day.

Tom Healey
Dramaturg

desert, 6:29pm was first produced by Red Stitch Actors' Theatre, Melbourne, on 22 November 2017, with the following cast:

ABBY	Ella Caldwell
JAMIE	Darcy Kent
RICO	Joe Petruzzi
XAN	Eva Seymour
CRYSTAL	Sarah Sutherland

Director, Bridget Balodis
Dramaturg, Tom Healey
Set & Costume Designer, Romanie Harper
Lighting Designer, Amelia Lever-Davidson
Composer & Sound Designer, Ian Moorhead
Voice Coach, Jean Goodwin
Stage Manager, Genevieve Davidson

This play was developed through Red Stitch's INK new playwriting program, proudly supported by the Malcolm Robertson Foundation and the City of Port Phillip.

CHARACTERS

CRYSTAL, mid 40s. She doesn't feel 40. She's only just begun to show signs of ageing, and it's terrifying. She feels old and ugly for the first time in her life. She placed a lot of value on her looks in the past, and with them fading she's frantically searching for a new source of self-worth. Manager of a bottle-o.

RICO, mid 40s. Was the popular rebel in high school. Is the popular former rebel now. His sense of humour was daring in high school, but now it's usually just crude. Has no filter, enjoys making people feel uncomfortable. He has never really struggled. No-one really close to him has ever died. He's worried this streak can't last.

JAMIE, 23. Brilliant but lazy. He's sarcastic and generally angry, hates being told what to do. Went to TAFE for a degree in information technology but gave up after a year and half when it got a little bit hard. He was, at one point, the great hope for the family: the smart one who was gonna do big things. He believed it too, and felt betrayed by the world when he realised he was just another human being. Listens to a weird combo of metal and Joni Mitchell.

XAN, 17. Still figuring herself out. She's got a drive that her brother does not. Very realistic, a hard worker, brave. She's never really fitted in, a loner, but up to this point is not bothered by it. She lacks direction, so her final year of school has been scary. She has suddenly realised that she feels uncomfortable in her hometown as an adult. Gay. Closeted. Loves junk food.

ABBY, 37. Grew up in Brisbane. Got pregnant really young and worked hard to support her daughter and put herself through school. Moved to this middle-of-nowhere town for work and simplicity and loves it. Her daughter is out of the house now, so she is experiencing a freedom and loneliness she never had in her youth. A bit of a control freak.

SETTING

A small town in the middle of nowhere. The desert. Present.

NOTES

A slash / indicates the point of interruption that the following line begins.

Moments marked as [*FANTASY*] take place in the character's head. These moments are internal. They are speaking to themselves, not the audience. The fourth wall is solid.

This play was originally conceived with the directive that the set should be the front exterior of a house, and all action should be viewed through a large set of sliding glass doors that lead to the inside of the house. Because of the literal fourth wall through which the audience would watch the action, the actors would be on mic, allowing their performances to be small, contained—the audience made aware of every tiny detail. While this is the ideal staging scenario, alternate design choices may be made to fit the needs/scope/reality of a production.

An unremarkable house. It's a comfortable but ugly house. Mismatched furniture, carpet, a little worn from being lived in for over twenty years, fingerprints on the walls. We are in the dining/lounge area. There's a television which the family can see from their spots at the dining table. During pre-show it should be on but unobtrusive, the audience can hear the murmur of it and see the light flicker.

Before the show starts XAN *enters from outside. She is wearing a Target uniform. She carries a plastic Target bag which she sets on the dining table. She sits and watches TV for a bit.*

FANTASY:

A spotlight on RICO *standing on the roof. He is a rock god. A karaoke backtrack plays. He sings a Guns N' Roses song. He's pretty good.*

At some point, Xan turns the TV off. She exits to her bedroom.

The song finishes.

FANTASY ENDS.

Blackout.

5:41PM

Lights up.

CRYSTAL *is sitting at the dining table, staring at the floor. She is completely still.*

FANTASY:

CRYSTAL: And it's me at this bar and I've had a bad day and stopped in for a gin and soda, which I never do, but this day had it in for me and I'm in a rough enough mood to sit alone at a bar and so I am and this man sits next to me and he orders a drink and then we sit there drinking for a while, nothing happens, but he keeps glancing over, and then finally, finally says, 'Are you Crystal?', and I'm like, 'What? How …', and he's all, 'Gav'. And I'm like, 'What?' And he's all, 'Gavin75'. And then I know, I know who he is, and what we've, and yeah I always figured his pictures were fakes and he was probably a twelve-year-old kid, but no, he's him, and he's here, and he's pretty hot, and we start talking and it's just … huge, it's a huge sparkly conversation and then he says, 'Want to go for a walk', and we get into his truck and drive out to the dirt and start walking, and it's a full moon, and it's a perfect temperature and we talk and talk and walk and walk and then we stop talking but keep walking and then he grabs my hand and stops me and he pulls me around to face him and I say, 'Should we?', and he says, 'I have to', and I say, 'Me too', and he says, 'Okay', and I say, 'Yes', and he kisses me and kisses me and kisses me and kisses me and we lay down in the sand and he takes off his pants—

XAN enters. She has changed out of her work clothes. She walks across the dining room and exits into the kitchen.

No. He takes off his shirt, he takes off his shirt in that way where he grabs the back of it and pulls it over his head and then he pauses and looks at me and starts unbuttoning my dress, it's my black dress from three years ago and it fits me 'cause I've lost some weight, and I just stare up at him in amazement and he puts his arm under my back and pulls me up and, and he unbuttons his pants with one hand and then … his face is still and he is silent as the desert and I …

XAN comes back in with a bag of snakes. She sorts through the colours trying to find the red ones.

And then we lay there, in the sand, me in his arms, and then the sun rises, and he picks me up, and carries me, to a new house, where I live an organised life, where I do yoga every morning at eight-thirty a.m., and drink lattes in large takeaway cups while I walk around a lake with my little dog and my good friends, and look up healthy recipes online to cook that night with a glass of sauv blanc in my hand. And then I open my eyes and I'm in my work uniform and the paint is peeling and I haven't vacuumed yet and my fingers smell like my vagina. I hate these pants.

FANTASY ENDS.

XAN is staring at CRYSTAL.

XAN: What are you—?
CRYSTAL: Huh?
XAN: What are you doing?
CRYSTAL: Sorry.
XAN: Mum.

CRYSTAL: No, yeah, sorry. I'm trying to decide if I should vacuum.

Pause.

I mean it's just Jamie. So, yeah. Who cares?

XAN: Totally.

CRYSTAL *looks at the Target bag.*

CRYSTAL: What's this?

XAN: I bought it for this weekend.

CRYSTAL: From work?

XAN: Yeah. I figured we could play it with Jamie.

CRYSTAL *opens the bag and pulls out the game Uno.*

CRYSTAL: Uno. Don't we have this already?

XAN: I couldn't find it.

CRYSTAL: It's in the hall cupboard.

XAN: No, I looked.

CRYSTAL: Well, it's nice to have a new deck anyway. Jamie will be happy.

XAN: Uh, no he won't. He hates Uno.

CRYSTAL: He doesn't hate it!

XAN: He definitely hates it.

CRYSTAL: You're making this up.

XAN: I'm not! He gets so angry when we play. He's always like, 'There's no strategy, this game is for infants, there's no strategy, and I hate you all'.

CRYSTAL: I guess how could a pack of cards compete with an Xbox.

XAN: It's so funny, I can't wait.

Pause.

CRYSTAL: Yeah. I'll just do it tomorrow.

XAN: What?

CRYSTAL: We can vacuum tomorrow. I just seriously can't right now. I'm so—God, I'm so tired I kept taking little naps standing up at work all day—like a, like a horse. I swear I'm only awake right now 'cause of Jamie.

XAN: Why are you so tired?

CRYSTAL: Early doctor's appointment, remember? I told you. Mammogram. You'll have to do them eventually. They put your boob in this machine and then they smash it hard—

XAN: Oh, my God.

CRYSTAL: You have to get them done starting at forty.

XAN: And the doctor like touches your chest?

CRYSTAL: Well, yeah.

XAN: Gross.

CRYSTAL: It's medicine, Xan. It's not gross. It's so I don't die of breast cancer. Jesus.

> *Pause.*

XAN: Are you like … wearing a lot of make-up?

> CRYSTAL *gets squirmy and embarrassed.*

CRYSTAL: What? No.

XAN: You look weird.

CRYSTAL: Do I? Do I look weird?

XAN: A little bit.

CRYSTAL: How? Unnatural?

XAN: Unnatural?

CRYSTAL: Orange? Or something.

XAN: Yeah, maybe. A little orange.

CRYSTAL: Right.

XAN: Are you okay? Maybe you're sick.

CRYSTAL: No, Xan, I'm not sick.

XAN: Remember how Rachel's sister got hepatitis? And apparently, / Rachel said she turned yellow.

CRYSTAL: No. Oh God, no. I don't have hepatitis.

> *Pause.*

I got a spray tan.

> XAN *is baffled by this.*

XAN: Why?

CRYSTAL: I don't know.

> *Pause.*

So it looks bad?

XAN: Um …

CRYSTAL: You said orange.

XAN: No, *you* said orange

CRYSTAL: So it looks fake?

XAN: It looks darker.

CRYSTAL: Tanner?

XAN: I mean—yeah. Tanner.

CRYSTAL: They said this was a very subtle natural shade, but I've been just freaking out all day that I look ridiculous. Do I—is it just ugly?

XAN: Um. No.

CRYSTAL: So you like it.

XAN: I just don't understand why you would, like—why get a spray tan?

CRYSTAL: I don't know, there's a place across from BWS, and it was only thirty dollars— I thought it would cost a lot more— and so I just … I just wanted to, you know, feel sort of pretty, or like … less globby, I guess.

Pause.

What else?

XAN: What?

CRYSTAL: It's chocolate, right?

XAN: Mum. Oh, my God.

CRYSTAL: What?

XAN: What are you talking about?

CRYSTAL: Your favourite kind of cake. So touchy.

XAN: You can't just change subjects without like telling the person you're having a conversation with. I'm a not a mind-reader.

CRYSTAL: That's how conversation works, Xan. What do you want? Like an announcement over a loudspeaker?

XAN: No.

CRYSTAL: *I'm changing subjects now. Prepare.*

XAN: Yes, that's what I want.

CRYSTAL: Anyway, what was I saying? Oh, that your father got sponge cake. I told him you wouldn't like it. You like chocolate though, right? Everybody likes chocolate.

XAN: You got me a cake?

CRYSTAL: Yeah, for graduation.

XAN: I'm not graduated yet.

CRYSTAL: But Jamie's coming in tonight so I thought we'd have a cake tonight.

XAN: Oh. Okay.

CRYSTAL: He said they were out of chocolate, but I bet he just wasn't paying attention.

>*Pause.*

What else?

XAN: What?

CRYSTAL: What else happened today?

XAN: Nothing. Just work.

CRYSTAL: That's life now that you've graduated. Just work.

XAN: I haven't graduated yet.

CRYSTAL: Well, yeah, but you've finished / school.

XAN: I don't graduate for a / week.

CRYSTAL: Yeah, but I'm just saying you're not in class. So now all that's left is work and it's just like—I personally found it very depressing when I realised that after you finish school all that's left is work.

XAN: Well.

>*Pause.*

I could go to uni.

CRYSTAL: Well. Yeah. That's true.

>Pause. Did you apply?

XAN: I'll probably apply next year.

>*Blackout.*

6:09PM

The television flicks on. Lights up.

RICO *and* XAN *are seated at the table, waiting. The table is fully set.* RICO *is watching TV.* XAN *is involved in her phone.*

FANTASY:

RICO: It starts with shitting blood.

>That's happened to me before, but it was nothing serious.

>And apparently most adults have this problem at some, at some point in their lives so, yeah, it often goes ignored.

>I Googled it.

>So I shit blood and then my belly starts to hurt all the time and I get

really weak and tired and I start losing weight. Then maybe I go to the doctor and he says, 'Well, it doesn't look good'. No. No, he says, 'I want you to stay calm until we know more. We need to do some tests.' And they stick a camera inside my asshole and they find the cancer, and they tell me that I'm going to have to undergo treatment. Yes. Treatment. Chemotherapy. Chemotherapy and radiation. But. But my chances aren't good so I refuse treatment, because I say I don't want my last days to be me sick as a fucking dog. So I just hold it. I hold it all here [*a gesture*] until I can't. Yes. And I'd be in more and more pain. And one day Crystal would find me trying to keep it together in the bathroom. Bedroom. No. In the bathroom. And she'd be like, 'What's wrong, should I call an ambulance?' And I'd be like, 'We don't have ambulance cover, leave me the fuck alone, I'm dying.' And it would hit her for the first time, that after this, after this she was gonna be alone, without me. And it would destroy her. Like a little bird hit by a ute. And I'd have to carry everyone, my sad, sad family, on my back. And I would. I would carry them. I would pile them up and walk to the funeral home. And eventually it would get so bad that I'd be in one of those beds, like a hairless cat with bruises for eyes, shitting and vomiting and everyone would be crying and it would smell weird. And they would just be staring at me like 'fix it' and I'd be white-knuckling it until I couldn't anymore and then I'd die and burn in hell with all my least favourite people.

Yeah.

So I check always. I always take a good long look in the bowl— you want to check for changes in consistency because that could save your life.

Yeah, and I'm gonna start exercising again, because Brendan O'Connell. Yeah. He's dead now.

FANTASY ENDS.

XAN *raises her phone and snaps a photo of* RICO.

RICO: What are you doing?

XAN: The expression on your face. You looked terrified.

RICO: You have to warn me. I wasn't ready.

XAN: Yeah, that's the point.

RICO: Take another one.

XAN *raises her phone to take another,* RICO *lifts one side of his shirt revealing a nipple and makes a face.*

XAN: Gross, what are you doing?!
RICO: Take the photo!
XAN: No!
RICO: Take the photo!
XAN: I don't want to remember this moment.
CRYSTAL: [*offstage*] Is that?
RICO: [*still posing*] Come on!

CRYSTAL *enters abruptly, she's wearing different pants.*

CRYSTAL: I thought—
RICO: What?
CRYSTAL: I thought I heard a car pulling up.

RICO *listens.*

RICO: Your mum's hearing things again, Xan.
CRYSTAL: No, I thought I heard—no, no it's nothing.

Pause.

Wait, no, it's definitely—

She goes to the window.

Yeah, it's definitely a car. It's, wait. No it's not. It's not him. It's a yellow car. No, wait, what? What? It's stopping. It's, what? It's. Who could it? Did Jamie get a? What? Did he get new car? Xan?
XAN: Dunno.
CRYSTAL: He would have told us.
XAN: Maybe.
CRYSTAL: He's parking. It's him, he's parking the car. Turn off the TV, Rico, why wouldn't he tell us that? A new car?
RICO: So it's him?

RICO *walks to the window to stare out at the car.*

CRYSTAL: Yes, it's him. Turn off the TV. Xan.
XAN: I'm not the one watching it.

Silence. RICO *and* CRYSTAL *are looking out the window.* XAN *gives a passive aggressive sigh before begrudgingly finding the remote and turning off the TV.*

RICO: How'd he get that?

CRYSTAL: That's what I've been asking.

RICO: And why yellow?

CRYSTAL: I know.

RICO: Probably selling drugs.

CRYSTAL: If he's selling drugs he should use the money to buy phone credit instead of borrowing money off us.

XAN: Her parents stared out the window in horror at the yellow car.

CRYSTAL *and* RICO *look at* XAN.

They looked towards their daughter disapprovingly.

CRYSTAL: Xan.

XAN: Said Mum.

CRYSTAL: Stop it.

XAN: Mum continued.

CRYSTAL: I hate this. It's not funny.

XAN: Mum insisted, but deep inside, Xan knew it was funny.

RICO: I think it's funny.

XAN: Dad also knew it was—

JAMIE *enters, holding an Xbox.* XAN, CRYSTAL *and* RICO *stop what they are doing and look at him.* JAMIE *freezes.*

CRYSTAL: Do you have a bag?

JAMIE: Uh-uh.

CRYSTAL: But you're staying the night, right?

JAMIE: I'm staying the weekend.

CRYSTAL: Where's your stuff?

JAMIE: Stuff?

CRYSTAL: Yeah. Your clothes.

JAMIE: Didn't bring any.

RICO: Jamie's gonna let it all hang out!

Silence. No-one laughs.

JAMIE: I have an extra t-shirt in the boot.

XAN: We haven't eaten.

CRYSTAL: We were waiting for you.

Pause.

JAMIE: I'm gonna go to the toilet.

RICO: Yup.

> JAMIE *exits. They stand in silence and wait for him to pee. You can hear it. It's weird. He comes back. They are all staring.*

JAMIE: Are we waiting for something?
XAN: We were just waiting for you to finish in the toilet.
JAMIE: Ah.

> *Blackout.*

6:18PM

Lights up. CRYSTAL, RICO, XAN *and* JAMIE *seated at the table eating. About fifteen seconds of silent eating.*

JAMIE *gets up, goes to the kitchen, comes back with a bottle of salad dressing. He opens it and puts an unusually large amount of dressing on his salad.*

RICO: Jamie's having a little salad with his dressing.

> JAMIE *puts the top back on the bottle and starts to eat his salad. Silence.*

XAN: Can I have some?

> JAMIE *passes her the bottle.*

RICO: It's like—can I get you a spoon?
CRYSTAL: As soon as he walks in the door you start teasing.
RICO: He's fine. He's got a plate full of Caesar to make him feel better.

> *Silence.*

CRYSTAL: What else?
XAN: Uh. How's work?
RICO: Who, me?
XAN: No, Dad.

> XAN *looks at* JAMIE. *He looks up from his plate as if this question is shocking.*

JAMIE: Work's fine.
CRYSTAL: Good.

> *Silence.*

XAN: How's your … like … computer games?

JAMIE: Fine.

XAN: Are you winning?

JAMIE: I dunno.

XAN: What's it called? Aliens Versus People?

JAMIE: It's more complicated than that. You're thinking of Halo. But I play a wide array of games.

XAN: Yeah, but that's your favourite, right?

JAMIE: I don't have a favourite, but it's one I play frequently, I guess.

Silence.

CRYSTAL: Xan bought Uno cards.

RICO: We already have them.

XAN: No. I couldn't find them.

CRYSTAL: Anyway, we can play later.

XAN: [*to* JAMIE] You love Uno.

JAMIE: Right.

Pause.

CRYSTAL: What else? I couldn't find my keys this morning. Do you remember this, Xan? Do you remember me yelling? You were asleep and I came into your room and asked you if you'd seen them? Do you remember?

XAN: Yeah. I'm not like tracking your keys, Mum.

CRYSTAL: Yeah, no, I know, but, you might have seen them or something.

XAN: Pretty much if you lose your keys, it's your own fault, and the answer to where they are is, like, inside you.

CRYSTAL: Anyway, I finally found them.

Pause.

XAN: Where were they?

CRYSTAL: In the kitchen. Yeah. By the kettle. Under the edge of that— you know the—tray of—

XAN: Yeah.

Silence.

CRYSTAL: And so yeah, went to the doctor, did that, and then went to work, no stopped to get petrol, which was really expensive, and then went to work, and yeah, yeah, no it was fine. Sara had the day off because of her husband's foot surgery—because Sara usually works Fridays—but yeah, she wasn't there, instead Janelle was working and she's sorta, like, sorta new, I mean she's been working there for probably a month but only one day a week—we hired her because she's friends with Val—but she doesn't work that much—because she's—well, I don't really know why, or maybe she has a second job or something—she must have a second job, I don't know how anyone could work only one day a week—and so she doesn't really know what she's doing.

Pause.

Yeah.

Pause.

She dropped a case of wine. And she didn't know where the mop was—like hello? It's in the cupboard—

FANTASY:

CRYSTAL's *rant becomes muffled and blurred.* JAMIE *is alert, looking around the room.*

VOICEOVER: Defend our carrier.

JAMIE *takes a giant blue and orange machine gun from under the table. He stands up.*

VOICEOVER: Find our flag.

VOICEOVER: Our flag's been taken.

JAMIE *aims and fires. He misses. He fires again.*

JAMIE: We gonna have a problem here, bro?

He fires again. He misses. He stays calm and tracks his target around the room.

I'm gonna end this. I'm gonna end this. I need to end this. Oh, I can end this.

CRYSTAL: —the cupboard with the sign on it that says 'cleaning supplies'— so I had to show her that. What else? It was pretty quiet. 'Cept for that case of wine. And then I got off and stopped to see your Auntie Carol because she and Dave just got a new shed in the backyard. It looks good. It's bigger than I thought. They haven't moved anything into it yet. But yeah, it looks good. I told them they should paint it—

He fires again. He hits his target. It is practically orgasmic.

Yes. Oh my God. Yes. Bro.

    Yes.

    CRYSTAL*'s voice returns to normal.*

CRYSTAL: —because it's like this beige colour that doesn't match the house, but they don't seem to care, so I think they'll probably just leave it, which is, you know, it's their life, so that's fine.

XAN: What about the ssshhhhhhh?

    XAN *makes a spray-paint noise and gesture.*

CRYSTAL: What?

XAN: You know.

CRYSTAL: Oh, God Xan. Did you notice Xan's hair, Jamie? Half shaved. Just half.

XAN: Oh, my God, Mum, let it go.

JAMIE: I noticed.

XAN: Lots of people shave their heads.

JAMIE: You look like a lesbian squirrel.

XAN: What does that even mean?

CRYSTAL: You don't look like a lesbian squirrel.

JAMIE: No, you do. You look exactly like a squirrel if that squirrel were like a big dyke.

CRYSTAL: Jamie, / you're being silly. He's being silly, Xan, you're not a lesbian.

XAN: Jamie, that doesn't make sense. What you're saying doesn't make sense. I know you think it's like an insult, but it like literally makes no sense at all.

JAMIE: No, no, sorry, just like a lesbian. Like a lesbian human.

RICO: I like it. I think it looks good.

CRYSTAL: Really? You like it?

RICO: Yeah. I like it.

CRYSTAL: Okay.

    Silence. Eating.

What else?

    Blackout.

6:25PM

Lights up.
They eat silently for about thirty seconds.
Blackout.

6:27PM

Lights up.
They are still eating.

JAMIE: So what happened to the chooks?

XAN: Jamie!

JAMIE: What?

XAN: I don't know. We're like … eating chicken.

JAMIE: Right …

XAN: It's just like … a conflict of interest …

CRYSTAL: The chooks are dead.

JAMIE: Oh.

XAN: Jamie took the news surprisingly well considering he had a fair bit of chicken corpse currently inside his mouth.

JAMIE: What?

CRYSTAL: She does this all the time now.

XAN: He looked around confused as he ground the flesh to a paste with his teeth.

CRYSTAL: Uh. God. Stop.

XAN: Exclaimed Mum.

CRYSTAL: Xan, please.

XAN: Mum gave Xan a look that could kill fish.

CRYSTAL: Stop.

XAN: Mum—

CRYSTAL: *Stop it.*

XAN: Xan stopped.

CRYSTAL: The chooks are dead. Not sure why. They just died. Like house plants.

RICO: I think it was because of the heat.

CRYSTAL: No. No.

RICO: I think it was because of the heat.

CRYSTAL: The neighbours still have theirs. We were doing something wrong.

Ohmygod! Did you guys hear?

RICO: About the refinery?

CRYSTAL: What? No. About the girl. And the overpass.

XAN: Are you talking about last year when that old lady got caught with no pants on the highway and—?

CRYSTAL: What? No. I can't believe you haven't heard this. It just happened this morning. Her name's Josephine?

RICO: I don't know her.

CRYSTAL: She was the one with like … [*an incomprehensible gesture*] You know? She would always wear those like … that … like … what do you call it? Train punk?

JAMIE: What?

CRYSTAL: You know like … that style, they call it train punk?

RICO: No. What?

CRYSTAL: Yeah. With. Um. Goggles?

RICO: Steampunk.

CRYSTAL: Yes! Steampunk! It's steampunk.

XAN: Jo?

CRYSTAL: Yeah, something like that.

JAMIE: Jo? Yeah. I know her.

XAN: No you don't.

JAMIE: Yeah I do. I worked with her at EZ Video the summer after I graduated. I trained her.

XAN: So what happened?

CRYSTAL: She jumped off the overpass.

JAMIE: Whoa, what?

CRYSTAL: Yeah.

XAN: Is she okay?

CRYSTAL: Well. No.

XAN: What do you mean?

CRYSTAL: Well. She's in the … uh. Intensive care?

Pause.

XAN: Oh.

CRYSTAL: Were you friends?

XAN: No. I don't really know her.

JAMIE: Oh. I thought—

XAN: I like know who she is, but we aren't like friends.

JAMIE: Really?

XAN: You're being weird.

JAMIE: You're being weird.

CRYSTAL: I can't even imagine what her family must …

RICO: Well. Do they know what happened?

CRYSTAL: No. No note. That's what I heard.

JAMIE: So. It was. Like. On purpose?

CRYSTAL: I think so.

XAN: Where did you even hear this?

CRYSTAL: At BWS.

XAN: Who?

CRYSTAL: A customer. Sheryl.

RICO: The one that buys a bottle of Jack every second day.

CRYSTAL: Bacardi.

XAN: She's not reliable.

CRYSTAL: No, she's related to them. Cousin, or something.

JAMIE: Jo was a psycho.

RICO: Don't say that.

JAMIE: She was! At EZ Video she like—she would always get in trouble for dressing weird. She would like put glitter on her pimples instead of make-up.

RICO: Xan used to do that.

XAN: Everyone used to do that. It was dumb.

CRYSTAL: I didn't know you worked with her.

JAMIE: Just for like a few weeks though. She actually got fired for like … I don't know … just not doing anything.

RICO: You shouldn't say bad things about her when she's in hospital.

JAMIE: They're not bad. They're just true. I mean, it's not like being a like star employee at EZ Video is a good thing. I mean, I thought she was cool. She used to do funny things like sneak up behind customers and see how many M&Ms she could drop into their purse or whatever before they noticed.

Do you remember this, Xan?

XAN: Why would I remember this?

JAMIE: What are you talking about? Because you were there visiting me and she got like ten in the hood of your jacket and you like *freaked out*. Remember?

XAN: No.

JAMIE: What? Yes you do. You screamed like they were spiders or something and like had a little fit in the middle of the store. And then you wouldn't let me tell that story for like five years because you were so embarrassed.

CRYSTAL: Xan, you have to eat your dinner if you want dessert.

JAMIE: What, is she four years old?

CRYSTAL: She lives on lollies and chips. She's gonna to die of a heart attack.

RICO: Why wouldn't you leave a note?

CRYSTAL: I don't know.

JAMIE: Maybe she didn't have anything else to say.

CRYSTAL: Yeah, but think about Joanna's family.

XAN: It's Jo.

CRYSTAL: What?

XAN: There's no-one named Joanna here.

CRYSTAL: Whatever. I'm just saying, her family. They'd have no idea why, and God forbid she doesn't make it … I mean, it would just destroy you …

JAMIE: So you're saying when I decide I kill myself, be sure to leave a note.

CRYSTAL: Don't even joke about that, Jamie. I'm serious. I can't even … I feel really … She's only nineteen. She has her whole life … her whole life …

RICO: It's awful.

CRYSTAL: Why would anyone that young?

JAMIE: Because.

CRYSTAL: What?

JAMIE: It sucks here.

RICO: Nah.

JAMIE: What do you mean, it obviously sucks here.

RICO: Not enough to kill yourself.

JAMIE: Debatable.

RICO: It's what you make of it.

JAMIE: No. Ask Xan.

Pause. XAN *looks confused.*

FANTASY:

XAN: Xan's finger is barely touching her right arm.
She can see that they are touching but she can't actually feel it.
She can't feel anything.
It's trippy.

Her mother is eating salad in that annoying way.
Her brother is staring at her.
Stop.
Her father is doing that thing where he pretends his cutlery is drum sticks.
God, that's dumb.
He's so dumb.

I'm trying to remember.
But I can't.
Everything's just.

CRYSTAL: Xan. Seriously. Eat.

XAN: Xan tells herself to focus.
She takes a bite of chicken.
She lets it sit inside her mouth.
It's disgusting.
She spits it out into a napkin.

CRYSTAL: What are you / doing?

RICO: Don't do that.

XAN: She tries to make a list of everything that's bothering her.
But it's too big.
It's everything.
Just everything that's ever happened.
Everything ever in the history of history.
She's trying to remember a specific moment through the smoke of it all but terrible pictures keep popping up instead of the thing she's looking for.
A car crashing.
A plane crashing.
People screaming.

The end of the world.

A failed maths exam last Tuesday.

Every detail of the stupid room.

The television murmur.

No.

No.

It's your face.

That time that.

That time last year at Marissa Mancini's birthday party where you touch my right arm and say, 'Do you know if there's beer?'

You touch my arm.

You touch my arm.

My forearm.

My forearm here.

And the music is.

It's Drake.

It's not loud enough.

It doesn't feel like a party.

You touch my arm and say, 'Do you know if there's beer?'

And your face is just glowing.

But I pretend it's not.

And I say, 'Marissa's mum's right over there'.

Marissa's mum's right over there.

Like an idiot.

And your hand lands on my waist for half a second.

Your hand lands on my waist and I evaporate.

And now.

The clock on the wall. (It's about six-thirty.)

Also.

The stained carpet.

Xan acting weird.

Xan realising she should stop being a freak and say something.

Say something.

Say something normal.

Go.

FANTASY ENDS.

XAN: *Dad.* Dad. Why haven't you accepted my friend request?

RICO: What?

JAMIE: What?

XAN: On Facebook, Dad.

CRYSTAL: A friend request is— remember? I showed you it. It's like the thing in the upper corner you get a little red balloon and then it—the balloon has like a number in it—and then it shows the people that want to be your friend—if you click on it shows you the people. Remember? You became friends with Camille and Joshua?

RICO: I didn't see it.

JAMIE: I don't understand. Dad. Wait. You have Facebook?

RICO: Yeah, I know.

CRYSTAL: He doesn't have that many friends.

JAMIE: You mocked me for the past eight years about Facebook.

RICO: I just got it.

CRYSTAL: He got it last month.

JAMIE: Oh, it's on. Yeah, it's on now. What are you—like what are you gonna use it for?

CRYSTAL: What are you talking about? He's gonna use it for the same thing you use it for.

RICO: I'm gonna use it for online sex chats.

JAMIE: Dad. / Shut up.

RICO: I'm joking! I got it 'cause of Camille and Joshua. They have a message board to talk about karaoke nights.

CRYSTAL: Don't be disgusting.

JAMIE: Uh. What?

XAN: What?!

CRYSTAL: He means a group. They have a work group.

XAN: Dad. You don't sing karaoke. Oh, my God! I'm dying. I'm like literally gonna faint. Just like shoot me. Literally kill me. This is so hilarious.

RICO: It's just a pub. We go to the pub. After work we go to the pub. You know the pub over by the high school?

JAMIE: Yeah …

RICO: It's a pub, but sometimes on Thursdays they do karaoke. And we go on Thursdays. After work.

JAMIE: Wait. Do you sing?

RICO: Not really. Only sometimes.

XAN: This is so insane.

JAMIE: Yeah. It is. It's completely insane.

XAN: It's so insane I can't feel my hands.

JAMIE: Mum, did you know?

CRYSTAL: I mean I know about the pub, you always go to the pub on Thursdays. But you didn't tell me there was karaoke.

XAN: And you're not shocked? I am *shocked*.

CRYSTAL: Uh, no, why … why would I be shocked?

XAN: Dad *singing*? I'm like crying.

CRYSTAL: Why is that shocking?

JAMIE: It is *definitely* shocking.

CRYSTAL: Lots of people do karaoke.

XAN: I just can't imagine it. Can you imagine it?

JAMIE: Like how long have you been doing it for?

RICO: I don't know. Maybe a month or two?

XAN: *Wow.*

CRYSTAL: He's got a really good voice.

RICO: You haven't heard me.

CRYSTAL: Well, he used to. In high school.

XAN: Are you? Are you good, Dad?!

RICO: What?

XAN: Are you good?

RICO: I'm … well … yeah … I'm good I guess.

XAN: Sing something!

RICO: No way.

JAMIE: Yeah!

RICO: No.

XAN: You have to! Sing! Sing something for us now! Oh, my God—what do you sing? Like, what's your song?

JAMIE: Is it like—?

XAN: Tell us.

JAMIE: I bet it's like AC/DC.

XAN: Or like … what … like—?

JAMIE: Guns N' Roses?

XAN: No, it's John Mellencamp.

RICO: No.

JAMIE: Then what?

RICO: I don't know. Nothing. Whatever.

XAN: Come on, Dad, you have a song, everyone has a song, just tell us.

RICO: I don't have—

XAN: Is it like the Beatles or something?

JAMIE: No, it's 'I Will Survive'.

XAN: Yes, please let it be that.

JAMIE: Beyoncé?

XAN: 'Formation'? Or 'Hold Up'?

JAMIE: I can picture it Dad, and it's amazing.

XAN: He's like with a baseball bat and a yellow dress—

CRYSTAL: Oh God, it's not Beyoncé. Is it?

RICO: I don't have a song.

XAN: Just tell us! Why aren't you telling us? It doesn't matter. It's just a stupid song. It's not like the end of the world, Dad.

RICO: I don't have a song.

XAN: Is it Queen?

RICO: I don't have a song.

XAN: Wait. Is this a joke? Are you tricking us?

CRYSTAL: What are you talking about?

XAN: He's lying.

RICO: What?

CRYSTAL: Why would he lie?

JAMIE: Yeah, I don't think he's making this up.

RICO: I'm not lying.

CRYSTAL: So paranoid.

XAN: Just checking.

> XAN *pulls her shirt up over her face.*

CRYSTAL: When we were younger your dad wanted to be a full-on rock star.

RICO: What? No. Don't, seriously, that's not true—

CRYSTAL: It is true. You were always talking about starting a band and you even—

RICO: No, no, no, stop, that was just—I was just being eighteen. Like how Jamie's always taking photos.

JAMIE: What?

RICO: Oh—I don't / know—

JAMIE: I never said I wanted—I don't / take them to—

RICO: I just mean you're not gonna be a photographer.

JAMIE: Uh, I know. I didn't say I wanted to be a photographer.

>*XAN's shirt is still over her face.*

XAN: I've literally never met a photographer.

CRYSTAL: It's more like a hobby. It's not a job. What are you doing, Xan?

XAN: Nothing.

JAMIE: I know all that. It's a—yeah, it's a hobby.

>*Silence.*

CRYSTAL: Alright. I'll take your plates. Xan, you didn't finish.

>CRYSTAL *exits.*

>*FANTASY:*

XAN: She's thinking
>She's thinking about
>Half a piece of baked chicken.
>About dead animals.
>About meat.
>A beating heart.
>Suffocating.
>Disappearing.
>Your face glowing
>Like a streetlight.
>It's glowing like a streetlight
>But I pretend it isn't.
>The yellow car.
>*FANTASY ENDS.*

RICO: What?

XAN: Jamie.

JAMIE: What?

XAN: Tell us about your new car.

RICO: Is it a Toyota?

JAMIE: A Mazda.

RICO: Niiiiiice. Now. I've got one question for you.

JAMIE: What?

RICO: Can I have it?

JAMIE: Uh, no.

RICO: I'm just kidding. It's too girly for me. Weird colour. How much did it cost?

JAMIE: Oh, you know.

RICO: What like twenty? Twenty-five?

JAMIE: Something like that.

RICO: Moneybags over here is holding out on us, Xan. Did you rob a servo?

JAMIE: No.

RICO: You stole it?! He stole it!

JAMIE: My friend bought it.

RICO: Oh, so … What? I don't understand.

JAMIE: My friend bought it. And then didn't want it anymore.

RICO: He *gave* it to you?

JAMIE: Well. Yeah.

RICO: He gave you a car?!

JAMIE: She.

RICO: She? Jamie has a rich girlfriend!

JAMIE: She's my friend, and she just, you know, wanted to see it get driven. Because if you leave cars just sitting there for too long then—

RICO: Yeah, yeah I know. But that's … She's not your girlfriend?

JAMIE: No. She's older.

RICO: Ah. Okay. As old as me?

JAMIE: I don't know.

RICO: Just approximately.

JAMIE: I mean. I forget. I'd just be making up a number.

RICO: So why did—is she rich?

JAMIE: No. She's just normal. She's doing okay.

RICO: Is she pretty?

JAMIE: I don't know.

RICO: And you're not doing it?

JAMIE: Doing it.

RICO: The nasty.

JAMIE: Gross. Dad.

RICO: So why did she give you the car?

JAMIE: Because she wasn't using it.

RICO: Yeah.

> *Pause.*

I don't understand.

JAMIE: We're friends.

RICO: Yeah.

JAMIE: We hang out a lot.

RICO: You and the old lady?

JAMIE: We hang out and … I don't know … She knew that my car was a piece of shit and that I was having to spend all this money on it and stuff and so she just had this extra car sitting in the garage, because her daughter's at uni—

RICO: She has a daughter?

JAMIE: Yeah.

RICO: Did you date the daughter?

JAMIE: I never met her daugh/ter.

XAN: I feel sick. I think your chicken made me sick.

RICO: What? Really?

XAN: I'm going to lay down.

JAMIE: I feel fine.

RICO: Yeah, me too.

XAN: Well, I don't.

> XAN *exits.*

RICO: It was cooked through. I checked.

> CRYSTAL *enters with a cake lit with candles.*

CRYSTAL: Alright, here we—

RICO: She's in her room.

CRYSTAL: What, why?

RICO: She said she's sick.

CRYSTAL: She's not sick.

RICO: I don't know.
CRYSTAL: Well, shit. Do I blow them out?
RICO: Yes.
CRYSTAL: Isn't that bad luck?
RICO: No.
CRYSTAL: Xan?! Come here!
JAMIE: Why are there candles? It's not her birthday.
CRYSTAL: It's cake. I thought …
JAMIE: Just blow them out.
RICO: I'll do it.

>   *He does.*

>   *Blackout.*

7:08PM

Lights up.

XAN *on the roof with a blanket over her head.*
FANTASY:

XAN: Xan is still thinking about the night they were making out in the parking lot of KFC and they didn't even care if anyone saw them, except that they both really really did, and so they stopped so that they didn't get like … banished.

>   *During this* RICO *walks around the side of the house to take the rubbish out. He stuffs it in the bins. He stops. He looks at the sky. He sits on the ground and does nothing.*

And that's when Jo gave Xan this little plastic bag with a bow on it. It's a present, I mean. And Jo's face is glowing again and the light spills all over. And Xan feels like she might float away.
And Xan is like, 'what is this for?'
and Jo says, 'I don't know'
and Xan is like, 'that's weird'
and Jo says, 'open it'
and Xan is like, 'okay, but don't watch me'
and Jo says, 'why?'
and Xan says, 'too much pressure'
and Jo says, 'sure, whatever'

and it's a pair of sunnies

and Xan says, 'we sell these at Target'

and Jo says, 'I know, I stole them when I came to visit you at work last week'

and Xan says, 'hahahahaha'

and Jo says, 'what?'

and Xan says, 'please tell me you're joking'

and Jo says, 'about what?'

and Xan says, 'nothing'

and it gets really quiet

and then Xan says, 'you know I get ten percent off, and also I could have been fired'

and it gets really quiet again

and then Jo says, 'sorry'

and it was quiet

and Jo says, 'don't be mad'

and Xan says, 'it's fine'.

CRYSTAL *enters the dining room from the bathroom.*

CRYSTAL: Xan!

XAN: and then they get chicken

CRYSTAL: Xan!

XAN: well

I want you to know

I don't forgive you.

CRYSTAL: Where are you?

XAN: I'd come visit you in hospital, but that would be weird. But just so you know, when you get out, I'm going to punch you in the face for being a pathetic depressed hipster.

CRYSTAL: *Xan!*

FANTASY ENDS.

XAN: What?!

XAN *enters the dining room.*

CRYSTAL: Did you use my moisturiser?

XAN: What? No.

CRYSTAL: Why is my moisturiser on the bathroom counter?

XAN: What?

CRYSTAL: I always put it away in my drawer—that's why we each have a drawer— so we don't get stuff like this confused.

XAN: Ummm …

CRYSTAL: 'Cause, it's out on the counter. It's not in the drawer.

XAN: Sorry. I just—

CRYSTAL: Xan, this is sixty-three-dollar lotion for people with ageing skin, you're seventeen, your skin is— you're not having any skin problems, so I don't understand why you are using my sixty-three-dollar moisturiser.

XAN: I just had like dry skin and I didn't have any moisturiser or whatever. I didn't mean to like ruin your life.

CRYSTAL: I'm sorry, I don't want to be a bitch, but we've talked about this before and I just—

XAN: Right.

CRYSTAL: You're an adult now, you can be responsible for your own stuff—you've graduated.

XAN: *I haven't graduated.*

CRYSTAL: Well, we're having cake that says 'Happy Graduation Xan', so you're pretty close.

XAN: I didn't ask for cake. I don't like sponge.

CRYSTAL: No-one likes sponge, Xan, but it's the thought that counts.

> XAN *walks past* CRYSTAL *and out of the house.*

Are you serious?

> CRYSTAL *exits back into the bathroom to shower.* XAN *discovers* RICO. *He stands quickly. He's a little embarrassed for some reason.*

RICO: Xan my man!

XAN: What are you doing?

RICO: Just. The rubbish.

XAN: Oh.

RICO: And. It's, you know.

XAN: What?

RICO: A nice night. So I'm just. Hanging out.

XAN: Yeah.

RICO: Just for second. Do you …?

XAN: I'm like … I don't know.
    I'm like freaking out.

RICO *laughs.*

RICO: No you're not.

XAN: Yes I am.

RICO: You're totally fine. Everything is fine.

Pause.

Why are you freaking out?

XAN: Um. I just feel like—

Pause.

I don't know. Like I need to go to hospital.

RICO: Did you throw up again?

XAN: No! I didn't …

RICO: Okay, phew.

Pause.

So, then … What are you talking about?

XAN: Nothing.

RICO: Okay.

XAN: My arms are like itching. I think. I think I have a rash.

This freaks him out.

RICO: Want me to get your mum?

XAN: No. I want—

RICO: I bet you're just nervous about graduation or something. It happened to me once. I was at home alone and our neighbour was walking her dog—

XAN: I know, you told me this story before.

RICO: Oh. Yeah.

XAN: Yeah. And you had to call the ambulance.

RICO: Yeah.

XAN: The whole panic attack thing.

RICO: Right.

Silence.

XAN: I'm just …

Pause.

RICO: There's cake. Did you see?

XAN *doesn't say anything. She stands for a moment and then goes inside.*

RICO *looks at the ground. He tries to do some push-ups. He stops after about seven. He stands and dusts off his hands.*

The sounds of glass breaking in the kitchen.

CRYSTAL: [*offstage*] What was that?

A moment. More glass breaks. CRYSTAL *enters in a towel.*

Is everything okay?

CRYSTAL *goes into the kitchen.* RICO *comes back inside.* JAMIE *comes into the dining room. Another crash.*

[*Offstage*] Rico! Come here.

RICO: What is it?

CRYSTAL: [*offstage*] She's breaking things.

RICO: What?

CRYSTAL *comes into the dining room.*

CRYSTAL: I'm in a towel! She throwing bowls! What the fuck!

RICO: Why?

Another bowl breaks. A strange sob from XAN.

CRYSTAL: Because I told her not to use my stupid lotion.

CRYSTAL *and* RICO *exit quickly into the kitchen.*

I don't need this right now.

We hear some muffled talking. JAMIE *walks gingerly to the kitchen door and peeks in.* XAN *barrels out of the kitchen.* JAMIE *jumps out of the way.* CRYSTAL *and* RICO *follow.*

Did you break the blue trim ones? Xan. Where are you—where is she going?

RICO: Come on, Stal. Let's clean up.

CRYSTAL: This isn't my mess. This belongs to Xan. I'm not touching it.

Silence.

[*Sighing*] It's late.

JAMIE: It's seven-fifteen.

CRYSTAL: Oh. Well.

RICO: You guys wanna watch a movie?
CRYSTAL: No.

Blackout.

7:51 PM

Lights up.

XAN *and* JAMIE *watching TV.*

FANTASY:

JAMIE: If he was all, 'It's a fair wage', I'd be like, 'It's really interesting that you say that, Kaylen, because I happen to know for a fact that Hannah is being paid seventy-five cents more than me'. And then he'd be all, 'Have you been poking around in the back office?', and I'd be all, 'No, her pay slip was emailed to me accidentally last February, and the thing that confuses me, Kaylen, is that I have been working here for seven months longer than Hannah. Not only—'

JAMIE *pauses and gives a stern look.*

'You are gonna want to stop interrupting me right about now, Kaylen. 'Cause the thing is, Kaylen, not only am I am older, more knowledgeable about games, consoles, and the entire subculture of games really, I'm also over halfway to a Cert One in information technology. And I'm probably going back next year to finish. So really, Kaylen, I'm overqualified for this stupid fucking job. And. I want a raise. And I want more shifts. I'm done borrowing money from my parents to pay my stupid fucking phone bill, which I do use for business occasionally, so I feel like perhaps you should be paying a percentage of that, honestly. Now I don't want to quit and leave you hanging, but if you don't meet my very reasonable requests, I'm walking.'

Pause.

And then he'd be all, 'I'm sorry. There's protocol.' And I'd be like, 'Well, that's your last mistake'. And he'd be like, 'What do you mean my last—?', and I'd be like,

JAMIE *pulls out his giant blue and orange machine gun and fires.*

'Fuck you, Kaylen.'

FANTASY ENDS.

The doorbell rings. XAN *opens the door.*

ABBY: Hello.

XAN: Hello.

ABBY: I'm Abby.

　　Silence.

Sorry. Do I have the wrong house?

XAN: Yes.

ABBY: Oh, I'm sorry, do you know which one is number five four three—?

JAMIE: I'm here. Sorry. I'm here.

ABBY: There you are!

JAMIE: Yup. Hello.

ABBY: You ready?

　　CRYSTAL *enters.*

XAN: Ready for what?

ABBY: Oh. I thought we were going to Platinum.

CRYSTAL: You're going to Platinum?

JAMIE: I was gonna go later.

ABBY: You said eight. I swear you said eight.

JAMIE: Oh.

ABBY: [*looking at her phone*] See, yeah, I'm not crazy. I said, 'What about eight p.m?', and you said, 'Cool', and sent the thumbs up.

JAMIE: Sorry. Sorry. I thought you'd text me before you left.

ABBY: Oh. Sorry. I didn't know I was supposed to do that.

CRYSTAL: It's Xan's graduation party.

ABBY: You're graduating?! That's huge.

XAN: Not really.

ABBY: Look, we can seriously skip Platinum. I didn't realise—

JAMIE: No, we should go.

XAN: Go. I don't care.

CRYSTAL: Sorry, what's your name?

ABBY: Oh. Abby.

CRYSTAL: What?

ABBY: Abby.

CRYSTAL: [*calling off*] Rico, come meet Abby!

ABBY: You must be Jamie's mum.

CRYSTAL: [*calling*] Rico!

ABBY: It's Crystal, right?

XAN: The car?

CRYSTAL: What?

> RICO *enters.*

XAN: You're the—

JAMIE: She gave me the car.

ABBY: I loaned you the car.

JAMIE: Yeah. Loaned it. Obviously.

CRYSTAL: You loaned him a car?

ABBY: Yeah. The Mazda.

CRYSTAL: Why?

ABBY: My—

JAMIE: No-one was using it.

RICO: It's her daughter's.

ABBY: Exactly.

JAMIE: I'm gonna change my shirt real quick. This one smells like chicken.

XAN: Jamie's shirt smelled like—

CRYSTAL: Don't do that in front of guests.

> JAMIE *exits.*

RICO: Xan is unusual. I don't know if Jamie told you.

ABBY: No. Jamie didn't mention her being unusual. Are you unusual?

XAN: I'm just normal.

CRYSTAL: So you have a daughter?

ABBY: Rachel.

RICO: She's at uni.

CRYSTAL: How do you know this?

RICO: Jamie told me.

CRYSTAL: When?

RICO: Wanna sit down? Have some cake?

ABBY: Sure.

XAN: It's a sponge cake.

ABBY: I love sponge cake.

CRYSTAL: I'll get you a piece.

ABBY: My nanna used to make it for me.

CRYSTAL: Well, this one's from Coles.

CRYSTAL *exits to get some cake.*

ABBY: I feel like Jamie didn't tell you.

XAN: Tell us what?

ABBY: That we were going out.

XAN: Nope.

ABBY: Sorry.

XAN: For what?

ABBY: I don't know. Stealing him away.

RICO: Trust me, he's all yours!

CRYSTAL *enters with cake.*

CRYSTAL: Who's stealing?

RICO: Abby.

ABBY *laughs a little but no-one else does.*

ABBY: I just was just saying I'm sorry to be taking Jamie away from the party, but I promise to bring him back soon.

XAN: It's not a party.

CRYSTAL: So you gave him a car but you're picking him up?

ABBY: Designated driver.

CRYSTAL: That's nice of you.

ABBY: Oh, I'm not a big drinker, so it doesn't really matter to me.

RICO: Where are you going?

ABBY: Platinum?

RICO: Awesome!

ABBY: Oh, really? I hate it.

RICO: Oh, no, it's pretty cool, right?

CRYSTAL: When have you ever been there?

RICO: I've been there once.

CRYSTAL: When?

RICO: A few years ago.

CRYSTAL: For what?

ABBY: I mean, it smells like a toilet and the music's too loud, but what's the alternative? That pub by the high school?

RICO: It's not so bad.

ABBY: Have you been there on a weeknight? It's like desperate drunk people singing karaoke. You go in and you're like is this another universe?

RICO: Yeah.

ABBY: Anyway, we'll only stay for like an hour or something.

RICO: Cool, cool.

CRYSTAL: What else?

RICO: How do you know Jamie?

ABBY: [*with a little nervous laugh*] Oh, God.

RICO: What?

ABBY: No, nothing. We met online.

XAN: Online.

ABBY: Originally, I mean. We have hung out plenty in real life now, obviously.

XAN: Like Tinder or something?

ABBY: No. [*A nervous laugh.*] Actually it was this website message board thing.

XAN: What message board?

ABBY: It's, um. It's for board games?

XAN: Oh.

ABBY: I know it sounds lame. But I play a lot with Rachel and so I'm always, you know, looking for new games for, you know, birthdays and Christmas and whatnot, and on BGG—that's the website, BoardGameGeek—anyway, it has this thing where people review all the like newest coolest games.

RICO: Sounds useful.

ABBY: Oh no, it's *so* useful. I can't believe Jamie hasn't told you this, it's the craziest story.

XAN: What?

ABBY: Well. Okay. So on BGG all the best reviews were by this one person called brainpharaoh, right? And they were just like … these really like, I don't know, funny but also really like accurate and smart reviews. And I'd always read them and respond and like joke back or whatever and I guess we were like flirting a little, but I didn't really think anything of it because it was on this dumb website, right? But then. In this one thread brainpharaoh mentions that he lives only like forty minutes away from where my house is!

No-one really understands what's so exciting about this.

RICO: Oh. Wow.

ABBY: 'Cause I live all the way on the north side, and Jamie—well, you know where Jamie lives, obviously.

XAN: Yeah.

ABBY: And like. Well. It's an international website. People from all over the world comment on it. So that's just—seriously weird, you know?

RICO: Yeah.

ABBY: I figured brainpharaoh was in like Canada or something, not forty minutes away. Like, what are the chances?

XAN: You and brainpharaoh?

ABBY: Yeah. Well. Brainpharaoh is Jamie.

XAN: Brainpharaoh?!

RICO: Jamie has always loved games.

XAN: Oh, my God.

CRYSTAL: We always play Uno. He's vicious.

XAN: You can't be vicious at Uno.

CRYSTAL: Yes, you can.

RICO: So you're Jamie's girlfriend?

ABBY: Oh, God. I don't know.

CRYSTAL: How do you not know?

ABBY: Well, we haven't said that word. But. Sort of. I guess. I'm sort of his girlfriend. But not really. I don't know. Sorry.

CRYSTAL: Oh.

RICO: Jamie has a girlfriend! Call the paper!

ABBY: No. No. God. Don't call the paper.

RICO: No. I'm joking. I'm just joking.

ABBY: Sorry. We're just. Not using that word.

JAMIE *crosses the stage.*

JAMIE: I'm just gonna shave real quick and then we can go.

ABBY: Oh. You don't have to. It's not like … formal …

JAMIE: I'll be quick.

JAMIE *exits.*

RICO: He doesn't have much of a beard. Me, mine grows really fast and thick. I have to shave daily. Jamie, he's more like once every three or four days. But, you know. He's young. Maybe that will change. Although I've been like this since high school, haven't I, Stal?

CRYSTAL: I don't know.

RICO: Since I was fifteen I had to shave daily.

CRYSTAL: Right.

RICO: It's like, some people think that's a good thing, like it's a sign of a real man, but I say it's more of a pain in the ass than anything else, you know?

ABBY *laughs politely.*

ABBY: I guess so. I wouldn't really know though.

RICO: Well, I mean. You shave your legs and probably your privates, don't you?

CRYSTAL: What are you saying?   XAN: Dad, gross!

RICO: I just mean, you know how time-consuming shaving is. That's all I'm getting at. Sorry, I didn't mean to embarrass you. We're all adults here. I think we can be honest about this stuff—it doesn't have to be embarrassing. You shave your legs … I shave my face. You might shave other parts. That's fine.

CRYSTAL: Don't listen to him.

RICO: I'm just making conversation.

XAN: The worst conversation ever.

CRYSTAL: Did you hear about the girl who jumped off the overpass?

ABBY: Oh God, I know.

CRYSTAL: We're all praying for her.

XAN: We're not religious.

CRYSTAL: I just mean, we're hoping for her to get better.

ABBY: What? No. Sorry. But she …

Pause.

She died.

CRYSTAL: That's not what I heard.

ABBY: Yeah, no I think so. I'm pretty sure.

CRYSTAL: Oh, my God.

ABBY: I know.

RICO: Poor girl.

ABBY: They found the note, though.

RICO: Oh, good. I mean not good. Sorry. I mean awful—

CRYSTAL: What did it say?

ABBY: Well, this is just what my friend Kerri told me, so I don't really know, but she's a paramedic, and she said they found her ute. She had driven out into the dirt just off the road near the overpass and she had written in the dust on the window 'xoxo'.

CRYSTAL: 'xoxo'? What's that supposed to mean?

ABBY: Like hugs and kisses.

CRYSTAL: No, I know what it means, but that's her note? That's not a note.

ABBY: Well, I don't know, it's just what I heard.

CRYSTAL: No, that's not a note.

RICO: She probably didn't even write it. It was probably some dumb kid in the carpark of Woolies.

> JAMIE *enters.*

JAMIE: Ready?

ABBY: Great.

> XAN *punches the couch repeatedly—a nervous gesture taken too far.*

XAN: Jamie.

JAMIE: What?

XAN: It's my graduation party.

JAMIE: You said you didn't care.

XAN: Right.

JAMIE: Abby's already here.

ABBY: You can—

RICO: Let him have a night out, Xan.

XAN: *He has every night out.*

RICO: Just go, Jamie.

JAMIE: Okay. We're going. 'Bye.

CRYSTAL: Don't drink drive.

ABBY: Don't worry.

> *They leave. Silence.*

> CRYSTAL *looks incredulously at* XAN *and* RICO. *Silence.*

> CRYSTAL *looks at the floor, then back at* XAN *and* RICO.

RICO: What?

CRYSTAL: Nothing.

> *Pause.*

Just. Are you both like …?

> *Pause.*

Oh, my God.

RICO: What?

CRYSTAL: She has a grown child?

Pause.

I mean. She was way too old for him. Right? I mean, she must have been almost the same age as me.

RICO: I'm not great at guessing ages.

CRYSTAL: What is Jamie thinking?

Pause.

I just. I don't understand.

RICO *picks up Abby's plate. He stands for a moment, holding it. He exits into the kitchen.*

She gave him a car?

I mean, it's clearly not a physical thing. You know? Which is just. When I first saw her it was just like … You know? And then she said the thing about her daughter and I'm just sitting there like …

Jamie is a sweet, handsome, smart boy.

XAN: He plays video games like five hours a day minimum.

CRYSTAL: I mean. I'm just worried I guess. You know? He deserves a partner. Everyone needs someone, you know? A person to touch.

XAN: He has someone. We just met her.

CRYSTAL: Yeah, but not like … her. He's in his prime. He's just wasting it. And I'm just sitting here, watching him just … trying so hard and failing. I just … don't know what I'm supposed to do.

XAN: Nothing.

CRYSTAL: What?

XAN: Don't do anything. He'll figure it out.

CRYSTAL: But he won't. He won't figure it out.

XAN: Okay. Fine. He won't figure it out.

Hurt silence.

CRYSTAL: How can you say that?

Silence.

CRYSTAL *begins to cry.* XAN *does nothing.*

XAN: You're just desperate for attention.

XAN *turns on the TV.*

Blackout.

8:58PM

CRYSTAL *and* RICO *are watching TV.* XAN *calls from offstage.*

XAN: [*offstage*] *Mum.*
CRYSTAL: What is it?

> *No answer.*

> What is it?

> *No answer.*

> *What is it?*

> XAN *enters.*

XAN: I can't find my phone.
CRYSTAL: Well, I don't know where it is.
XAN: I need help finding it.
RICO: Maybe it's good for you. A little separation.
XAN: Can you call it? Please?
CRYSTAL: Here.

> CRYSTAL *hands* XAN *her phone.* XAN *dials. A ringing from offstage.*

XAN: Is it in your room?!

> *She gets it and comes back.*

> Why was it in your room?
RICO: Oh, sorry. That was me. I forgot. I put it on the charger.
XAN: I need you to not touch my stuff.
RICO: It was beeping.
XAN: Then just come get me.
RICO: You working for the government?
XAN: It's just manners.
RICO: She's working for the government.

> XAN *sits and looks at her phone.*

> Who are you texting?
XAN: No-one.

> *Pause.*

RICO: Facebook?

XAN *glares.*

CRYSTAL: I'm actually so grateful I grew up without the internet.

RICO: Tell me about it.

CRYSTAL: I mean, the thing was we had to be creative, you know, we had to find things to do.

RICO: We would do burnouts in the parking lot of Kmart.

XAN: Ugh.

RICO: What? It was fun. We weren't hurting anyone.

CRYSTAL: Remember when we did mushrooms out in the dirt, Rico? And you thought that box of Jatz was the funniest thing you'd ever seen.

XAN *covers her ears.*

XAN: Mum.

CRYSTAL: One day you'll be old, Xan, and you'll think, 'I wish I did more crazy things when I had the option'.

XAN: Like dating an older woman?

CRYSTAL: Well … that's not crazy. That's just not knowing what's good for you.

RICO: You know I dated an older woman once.

CRYSTAL: What?

RICO: In high school. She was a student teacher. Named April.

CRYSTAL: You didn't date her.

RICO: She was twenty-eight.

CRYSTAL: Oh, God.

RICO: I was fifteen.

XAN: Dad. That's like illegal.

RICO: Is it?

XAN: Yes.

RICO: Nah.

CRYSTAL: Don't tell this story.

RICO: She wasn't all that attractive. I mean she was kinda chubby, not that there's anything wrong with that, but she was always touching me, just on like the arm or the back during class. And then she asks me to help her take this box of books to her car, so I did, 'cause she was the teacher, and you gotta do what the teacher says, right, Xan?

CRYSTAL: No-one wants to hear this story, Rico.

RICO: Anyway, long story short, when we got to the car park she grabbed my, you know, and she had this van and—

CRYSTAL: No-one wants to hear this!

RICO: I thought we were talking about being crazy teenagers.

CRYSTAL: Not that story.

RICO: Okay, okay. Anyway, she's a lesbian now.

CRYSTAL: How do you know she's a lesbian?

RICO: She wished me happy birthday on Facebook this year.

CRYSTAL: What?

RICO: Yeah.

CRYSTAL: What'd she say?

RICO: Just happy birthday, that's it. I looked at her profile and she's a full-on lesbian. With like short hair and everything.

CRYSTAL: She's a psychopath.

RICO: Anyway.

CRYSTAL: What?

RICO: I'm just saying.

CRYSTAL: What?

RICO: I like Abby.

      CRYSTAL *looks at* RICO.

CRYSTAL: I'm going to bed.

1:04 A.M.

JAMIE *is setting up his Xbox.* ABBY *hovers.*

JAMIE: Okay, so it's set like five hundred years in the future. And there are all these colonies of humans throughout outer space. But—

ABBY: Are we gonna wake people up?

JAMIE: No, it's fine.

ABBY: Okay.

JAMIE: Actually, maybe we should be quiet just in case.

ABBY: Okay.

JAMIE: So anyway the colonies are like fighting, it's like civic war and there's—

ABBY: Civic war?

JAMIE: No. No. Sorry. Hahaha. No, I meant, I meant like—

ABBY: Civil war?

JAMIE: Yes. Sorry.

ABBY: Too much beer.

JAMIE: No. No. I just got tongue-tied.

ABBY: Okay.

JAMIE: So anyway, this woman called Catherine Halsey, she comes up with this like program to help keep the peace and everything—the Spartan 2 program—and they take kids and then like raise them to be soldiers and they like cybernetically enhance them—although that process killed lots of them—but the ones that made it through have this crazy armour which improves like their strength, speed, agility, and stuff.

ABBY: Is that like their skin? The armour?

JAMIE: No, it's over their body.

ABBY: Like an insect?

JAMIE: Yeah. Like an exoskeleton

ABBY: Basically like an army of Jason Bournes?

JAMIE: Yeah, like Jason Bournes with crazy armour as well. I can't believe you've never played it, it's like totally your thing.

ABBY: I don't really do video games, I'm too old.

JAMIE: Shut up, you're not old.

ABBY: Whatever, I'm a board game kinda girl. I don't have the hand-eye coordination for video games.

JAMIE: It's more than hand-eye coordination. There's strategy.

ABBY: Well, I've got strategy. I've got buckets of strategy.

JAMIE: I know, that's what I'm saying, you're gonna love it.

ABBY: We'll see. The backstory is already overwhelming.

JAMIE: No, no. It's okay. Look, here, watch this, it will make it all make more sense.

He plays the opening of Halo 5.*

ABBY: What's this?

JAMIE: It's the cinematic. Like a little story that plays before the game.

ABBY: It's so realistic.

JAMIE: I know.

ABBY: It's like a movie.

JAMIE: Amazing, right? I'm gonna get a beer. Do you want one?

---

* https://www.youtube.com/watch?v=Z43ZMBVgKWg)

ABBY: Ummmm … yeah … sure.

> *He exits and comes back with a bottle of Southern Comfort and two glasses.*

JAMIE: There wasn't any beer. This is all I could find.

ABBY: Gross.

JAMIE: Do you still want it?

ABBY: Sure, let's do it.

> *He hands her a glass. She takes a sip.*

Can we pause it?

JAMIE: Uh. Yeah. Okay.

ABBY: 'Cause I have a question.

JAMIE: Wait. Did you just say 'Christian' or 'question'?

ABBY: I said question.

JAMIE: Okay, 'cause I was like, 'What do you mean, you have a Christian?'

ABBY: No. I said question.

JAMIE: Okay.

ABBY: It's not about the game.

JAMIE: Okay.

ABBY: Okay.

JAMIE: Okay.

ABBY: Okay. So the question is. The question is did you not tell your parents about me?

JAMIE: Oh, right. Um. No. Not really. I didn't tell them. No.

ABBY: Right.

JAMIE: Yeah.

ABBY: That's what I figured.

> *Pause.*

So why didn't you tell them?

JAMIE: Oh. Um. I don't know. 'Cause it's. Just. 'Cause it's weird.

ABBY: How is it weird?

JAMIE: I don't know. It just like … feels weird. You know?

ABBY: No, not really.

JAMIE: It's just like … weird to like say that to your family. It's like …
I don't know … It's just weird and like kinda like gross, you know?

ABBY: Right.

JAMIE: I just mean that it's like none of their business.

ABBY: I mean it kind of is their business.

JAMIE: I just mean like … I'm my own person and they don't need to know every little detail of my life, like I'm an adult, you know?

ABBY: Okay. Fine.

JAMIE: What?

ABBY: I mean, yeah, you definitely don't have to tell them every detail of our relationship. But you could just mention that I exist, you know?

JAMIE: It's just not how I am. It's not … like …

ABBY: It's like common fucking decency.

JAMIE: Like what am I supposed to do? I'm just supposed to be like at dinner or something like, 'Mum, guess what, I have a girlfriend'.

ABBY: I mean, I don't care when you say it. If you don't want to say it at dinner that's fine. Call them if that's easier, or you could write it in a note if you need to, / that's not the point—

JAMIE: Ugh, I'm not gonna write a note, that's so gross.

ABBY: Okay *stop*.

JAMIE: What?

ABBY: You have to stop using that word.

JAMIE: What word?

ABBY: I'm not gross.

JAMIE: I'm not saying *you* are gross. I'm saying the *situation* is gross.

ABBY: *Are you—?!*

> She takes a deep breath, a calming technique.

I feel … like you not mentioning me to your family is just … really disrespectful. To me.

JAMIE: I didn't—

ABBY: And it makes me think that you would prefer I didn't exist except when, like, it's convenient for you.

JAMIE: What? No! You exist. You consistently exist, I like that you exist, I like that you consistently exist all the time.

> Silence.

I don't know what to do. I'm bad at this.

ABBY: Yeah, everyone's bad at this! But like … just like mentioning my name to your mother, that's not complicated.

JAMIE: Yeah … I've just … I don't know …

ABBY: What.

JAMIE: I've never like … had a … like a real girlfriend before or whatever. I mean I've definitely, I've definitely dated lots of girls, lots of women, but I never. I don't know. Had to like introduce anyone to my family or anything. So I just. I don't know what to do. Or whatever.

ABBY: Oh.

Okay.

I didn't know that.

JAMIE: So …

ABBY: That actually makes a lot of sense.

JAMIE: Yeah, well. Welcome.

ABBY: Welcome?

JAMIE: Yeah. Like. Welcome to who I am.

ABBY: What are you talking about?

JAMIE: Just. I fuck up a lot.

ABBY: Jamie.

JAMIE: So now you can just like join the rest of world and like grieve for me.

ABBY: What are you talking about?

JAMIE: Like, 'He had a Year Eight reading level in Year Three, bla bla bla, but he ended up a total loser anyway'.

ABBY: You're not a loser.

JAMIE: No. I am. I am a piece of shit.

Silence.

My internet got cut off yesterday.

ABBY: Oh.

JAMIE: I didn't pay the bill.

ABBY: Do you want to borrow some money?

JAMIE: I want you to punch me in the face.

Silence.

ABBY: Can I tell you something?

JAMIE: What?

ABBY: I haven't had a boyfriend since I was in high school. Not officially.

JAMIE: Frank.

ABBY: What?

JAMIE: What about that guy, Frank?

ABBY: Phil?

JAMIE: Yeah. You said you and him were—

ABBY: I mean, I know. I guess I was exaggerating. We were never really together.

JAMIE: Fuck Frank. Phil. Fuck that guy.

I think maybe I'm a little drunk …

JAMIE *goes horizontal.*

ABBY: I'm getting you some water.

She exits into the kitchen.

JAMIE *takes off all his clothes and lays back down.* ABBY *enters with a glass of water.*

There's a pile of broken glass in the corner—What are you doing?

JAMIE: Nothing.

ABBY: I feel like you should put your clothes on.

JAMIE: It's hot. This is my favourite glass. Did you know that?

ABBY: I didn't. I just gravitated towards it.

He drinks.

JAMIE: Xan broke the bowls. She was just throwing them against the wall and shit.

ABBY: Oh, my God. Why?

JAMIE: I don't know.

ABBY: I don't understand.

JAMIE: She like threw the bowls against the wall.

ABBY: And what'd she say about it?

JAMIE: Like … nothing.

ABBY: Well, did you try to talk to her?

JAMIE: She doesn't want to talk.

Pause.

ABBY: Right.

JAMIE: What?

ABBY: Drink your water.

JAMIE: You're so nice.

ABBY: Shush.

JAMIE: You're so nice and pretty and smart …

ABBY: You're just drunk.

JAMIE: I'm not that drunk.

ABBY: Okay.

JAMIE: I'm gonna tell my whole family about you. I'm gonna like make a banner, a big yellow banner that's like, 'Mum and Dad, this is Abby, she is so nice and so pretty'.

He kisses her.

I might actually be a little drunk.

ABBY: Yeah.

They kiss.

JAMIE: Like I might be too drunk to have sex.

They kiss more.

I'm sorry. I think I'm just too drunk.

ABBY: It's okay. That's okay.

JAMIE: Fuck. I'm sorry.

ABBY: No, no … it doesn't matter …

JAMIE: I hate myself.

ABBY: Look …

How about I touch myself?

JAMIE: What, like wank?

ABBY: Yeah. And you can watch.

JAMIE: Okay.

She puts her hand down her pants. A moment.

XAN *enters and watches blankly. Then she walks past* ABBY *and* JAMIE *and turns on the television.* ABBY *sees* XAN.

ABBY: Oh, shhhhhh—

JAMIE: What? What's wrong?

ABBY: Your sister.

JAMIE: Oh, God.

ABBY *and* JAMIE *fumble with their clothes.*

Can you hand me, hand me my pants.

ABBY: Shit.

JAMIE: Shit.

Xan.

You shouldn't—

You should be in bed.

They stand and stare at XAN *who stares at the TV.*

Xan.

ABBY *looks at* JAMIE.

JAMIE *doesn't know what to do. He folds himself into a little ball and tries to disappear. A moment.*

ABBY: Xan. I'm really sorry.

XAN *doesn't respond.* JAMIE *looks up.*

We shouldn't have been in the lounge room.

XAN *doesn't respond.*

ABBY *steps in* XAN*'s line of vision and bends down to look her in the eye.*

Xan.

JAMIE: What are you doing?

XAN *looks at* ABBY.

ABBY: I'm really sorry. We both are. Okay?

JAMIE: Stop. This is stupid.

ABBY: How is it stupid?

JAMIE: Or not stupid. Just like … I don't know. Like she doesn't know you.

ABBY: Okay …

JAMIE: Like. I'll talk to her.

ABBY: Will you?

JAMIE: Yeah.

Pause.

You should probably just go.

ABBY: Okay.

JAMIE: I'm sorry.

ABBY: Not a problem.

JAMIE: I'll call you tomorrow.

ABBY: Okay.

JAMIE: Sorry.

ABBY: Where's my phone?

JAMIE: I, ummm. I don't know. Do you. Want me to call it?

ABBY: No.

No, here it is. I've got it. Okay. 'Bye.

ABBY exits.

JAMIE: Shit.

JAMIE stands and watches XAN. XAN *watches TV.*

XAN: Can you get me those Pringles in the pantry?

JAMIE: Um. Sure.

He exits into the kitchen and returns with a can of Pringles.

XAN: Were there cheese ones?

JAMIE: I don't know.

XAN: Can you check?

He exits into the kitchen and returns with cheese Pringles. They both stare at the television for a while.

JAMIE: Have you seen the British version of this?

Nothing.

It's like a fuckton better. America ruins everything.

Nothing.

Abby might be mad at me. Do you think she's mad?

XAN: Why?

JAMIE: Because of … like … I told her to go?

XAN: She was the one being crazy.

Pause.

JAMIE: Um. So. Are you, like— okay?

XAN looks up.

XAN: I dunno.

JAMIE: Are you mad at me?

XAN looks back at the TV.

XAN: No.

JAMIE: Are you sure?

XAN: I'm just watching TV.

JAMIE: Okay. Just checking.

Pause.

Do you like ... remember when we were little?

XAN: What do you mean?

JAMIE: Like, do you remember being a little kid?

XAN: Obviously.

JAMIE: Like ... okay. Do you remember ... uh ... the CKC?

XAN: What?

JAMIE: It was, it stood for the Cool Kids Club? I mean. Fuck. It wasn't a real thing. So I did it to you and I did it to my friend Jared. Like, it was just something I made up, you know? It wasn't a real club. But you were like so little and Jared was ... I don't know, he was stupid or something—'cause you both believed me and you would like—just do whatever I said. I'd just be like, 'If you don't give me some of your Pringles you're not going to be in the CKC anymore', or whatever and it—

CRYSTAL enters half asleep in pajamas. JAMIE *goes silent.*

CRYSTAL: You're home. Great. I have to wee.

She exits into the bathroom and JAMIE *continues in a softer voice:*

JAMIE: —it literally always worked. I'm just saying I just used to be really, like, seriously *mean* to you. Like in so many ways. I would hurt you. And I guess, you know, actually, what it was, all of that, the fucking CKC ... like, it was just ... bullying ... and I just hope I didn't do any—like permanent damage. And I'm just sorry. You know?
       Xan?

XAN: What?

JAMIE: I'm sorry.

XAN: It's fine.

JAMIE: Okay.

XAN: I don't even know what you're talking about.

JAMIE: The CKC? Don't you remember? The CKC. The fucking CKC. I'd be like you can't join the CKC, Xan you're too little for the CKC, and you'd, fuck sometimes you'd cry, and I'd be all, 'Don't tell Mum or you'll never be allowed to join ...'

CRYSTAL walks back from the bathroom.

XAN: Doesn't it feel like we're just in a television show right now?

JAMIE: What?

XAN: Like, if you put like music behind what we're doing. You're like CKC, Xan, CKC, CKC! It would be hilarious. Or like tragic.

Pause.

I do that a lot.

JAMIE: What?

XAN: Pretend I'm in a TV show. Or like … a novel sometimes. Like, 'She felt like she was gonna vom but she kept eating Pringles anyway'.

JAMIE: Are you gonna vom?

XAN: No.

JAMIE: Okay, 'cause I can't handle vom right now. So just. Warn me.

XAN: I'm not gonna vom.

JAMIE: 'He couldn't handle vom right now, so he needed her to warn him.'

XAN is not impressed.

But, seriously. You know?

Nothing.

I'm like … asking for your forgiveness.

XAN: It's fine. I don't care.

JAMIE: I feel like shit. And I'm trying to get over it, but I've been having a lot of trouble forgiving myself.

XAN: Okay.

JAMIE: I'm just. I'm really trying to get my shit together, you know? But it's just … it's not easy. Abby told me one of the hardest things she ever had to do was forgive herself. And like … once she did, everything sort of clicked into place. 'Cause, you know … she had her daughter really young, so that was … I'm just … Maybe you're too young to understand what it's like. But things get … harder.

Silence.

XAN: She seems like a crazy bitch.

JAMIE is confused.

JAMIE: Are you talking about yourself in the third person?

XAN: I'm talking about your girlfriend.

JAMIE: You're fucked.

Pause.

You're just jealous.

XAN: Of what?

JAMIE: Of me having a girlfriend.

XAN: Actually. Maybe like … maybe it's your fault I fucked up my hair like this.

JAMIE: What?

XAN: Yeah. You were supposed to be like a male role model for me and instead you just bullied me. And so now I'm just like a … what was it? A lesbian squirrel? And so now you should just like lynch me.

JAMIE: What? No. I definitely don't want to lynch you …

Silence. XAN *stares at the TV.*

XAN: I've seen the British version and it's shit.

Blackout.

2:32 A.M.

Lights up.

XAN *is watching television alone. She looks up at the ceiling.*

Blackout.

3:16 A.M.

Lights up.

The television is on, but no-one is on stage. A moment. XAN *comes back from the kitchen with a block of chocolate. She sits and eats and watches.*

Blackout.

4:50 A.M.

Lights up.

XAN *is watching television. She turns it off.*

FANTASY:

XAN: She's thinking. She's thinking that if she could tell you one more thing, one last thing, it would be about yesterday when she was in line at the servo and there was this fucked-up lady in front of her buying like fourteen Cherry Ripes. And she's like paying for each one separately and keeping the receipts very methodically like it's an important business transaction or something. And yeah, so Xan's in line behind this woman, just *judging* her, just *hating* her, just thinking what a, what a, what a *crackhead*. And then the woman turns around and hands Xan a Cherry Ripe. And Xan says, 'Oh, … no … no thank you'. And the woman says, 'Are you allergic?' and Xan says, 'No', and the woman says, 'Do you hate fruit?' and Xan says, 'No, I like it', and the woman says, 'Then I want you to have this', and Xan says, 'No no, it's okay, I don't need it', and the woman says, 'I can't go into it all right now, but today is a really special day and I want to share it with you, so I want you to have this stupid piece of chocolate'. And so she takes the chocolate. And she thinks … 'Thanks'. And she thinks, 'Man, this town is weird'. And she thinks, 'I'm probably gonna be stuck here forever. I'm probably gonna be stuck. But. But I always thought that you, that you would get out. I always thought that you would get far, far away. And then one day you would come back in your broken ute and you would call me up and you'd say, "What are you doing?" And I'd say, "Nothing, I mean, I have a shift at Target later, but …" And you'd say, "Fuck Target. Get in." And I'd get in. And then you'd say, "Let's get the hell out of here".'

But I guess that's …

FANTASY ENDS.

She tries not to cry.

She turns the TV back on. She takes a bite of chocolate.

Blackout.

MORNING 8:36 A.M.

Lights up.

XAN *hasn't moved.* CRYSTAL *is drinking tea and looking at Facebook on a laptop.* RICO *enters and picks up a box of cereal on the table, he exits into the kitchen.* XAN *grabs the can of Pringles and eats a few.* RICO *comes back, still holding the box of cereal, with a confused look on his face.*

CRYSTAL: Use a mug.

JAMIE *emerges.*

You're up early.

JAMIE: No I'm not.

CRYSTAL: It's eight-thirty.

JAMIE: That's a completely normal time to get up.

CRYSTAL: You usually sleep way past—

JAMIE: I've been getting up at eight-thirty every day for like four months now.

CRYSTAL: Okay. Sorry.

> *Pause.*

Did you set an alarm or—?

JAMIE: Yes, I set my alarm.

> RICO *comes back with a mug and pours cereal and milk into it.*

CRYSTAL: Well, we don't mind if you sleep in here.

JAMIE: This is my routine now. Is there breakfast?

RICO: Cereal.

CRYSTAL: You have to use a mug though, 'cause Xan broke all the bowls. Wear shoes. There's glass.

> *Blackout.*

9:45 A.M.

XAN *is on her phone.*

XAN: Hi. Um. Can I speak to Meagan?

> Yeah, I can.
>
> Hi, Meagan, it's Xan.
>
> I'm a, um, customer service assistant?
>
> Yeah.

> RICO *enters.*

Um. Hang on. Sorry.

> XAN *exits into the kitchen, but we can still hear her, as can* RICO.

So. Um. I'm calling because I'm just getting, I think, I have like food poisoning? So I can't yeah, um, work today.

> Yeah, sorry.
>
> Okay.
>
> No, I'll be fine for tomorrow.
>
> Thank you.
>
> 'Bye.

XAN *comes back into the dining room.*

RICO: Who was that?

XAN: No-one.

RICO: Are you sick?

XAN: I'm fine.

> *Pause.*

RICO: Okay.

11:10 A.M.

Lights up.

XAN *is still sitting at the table.* CRYSTAL *is vacuuming around her.* CRYSTAL *turns off the vacuum cleaner.*

FANTASY:

CRYSTAL *looks at* XAN.

XAN: Oh, shit.

CRYSTAL: What?

XAN: I'm sorry, Mumma. I forgot to clean up all that broken glass.

CRYSTAL: Oh, that's okay.

XAN: I'll do it now.

CRYSTAL: I'll get the broom.

XAN: No, I got it.

> XAN *stands and walks towards the kitchen.*

Mum.

CRYSTAL: What's the problem?

XAN: Nothing.

CRYSTAL: Tell me.

XAN: Just. I'm sorry. For everything. I feel like I've taken you for granted.

CRYSTAL: I mean. I just—

XAN: You keep this whole family together. You do so much for all of us. And I just want to say thank you.

CRYSTAL: Well. You're welcome.

> *FANTASY ENDS.*

CRYSTAL: Xan.

XAN *looks the other way.*

Do you think this shirt looks bad on me?

XAN: I dunno.

Blackout.

1:44 PM

JAMIE *is unplugging his Xbox from the television.* XAN *hasn't moved from her spot.*

XAN: Where are you going?

JAMIE: Home.

XAN: You said you were staying two nights.

JAMIE: I got called in to work tomorrow morning.

CRYSTAL *enters.*

CRYSTAL: Where are you going?

JAMIE: Home.

CRYSTAL: You said you were staying two nights.

JAMIE: I got called in to work.

CRYSTAL: We were gonna order pizza from Mario's for dinner.

JAMIE: I don't want to drive in the dark.

CRYSTAL: You can't leave without having Mario's.

JAMIE: I have to.

CRYSTAL: And we were gonna play Uno. Xan bought a new deck. She was so excited about it.

JAMIE *looks at* XAN.

XAN: Do whatever you want.

RICO *enters.*

RICO: Where's he going? You said you were staying two nights.

JAMIE *gives an exasperated sigh.*

Blackout.

2:16 PM

The whole family is playing Uno. JAMIE *is not pleased. They are sitting in the following order:* JAMIE, CRYSTAL, XAN, RICO *(back to* JAMIE, *etc.).*

CRYSTAL: Whose go?

RICO: Mine.

CRYSTAL: So go.

RICO: I think I have to draw.

JAMIE: So draw.

RICO: I'm just making sure.

JAMIE: You only have seven cards. It can't be that hard.

>   RICO *draws. He stares at the card for a moment.*

CRYSTAL: It's either blue or it's not, Rico.

RICO: It's not.

CRYSTAL: So draw again.

JAMIE: No, you only draw once. It's my turn.

CRYSTAL: No. We've always played you keep drawing until you can put down.

JAMIE: That's not the rules.

CRYSTAL: It's how we've always played.

RICO: I'm sorry to say it, but she's right. House rules. Tragically, I have to draw.

>   *He draws again and stares.*

CRYSTAL: Oh, my God.

JAMIE: Seriously.

>   RICO *draws a third card. He stares at it for a moment.*

RICO: There we go.

>   *He plays it.*

>   *Blackout.*

2:20PM

Lights up.

CRYSTAL *is wearing a different shirt.*

RICO: Did you just change clothes?

CRYSTAL: Oh. Just my shirt.

RICO: Just making sure I'm not going insane.

CRYSTAL: Skip.

>   CRYSTAL *plays a Skip card.* XAN *sighs.*

[*To* XAN] Why are you so grumpy?

> *The sound of a text message.* JAMIE *picks up his phone and responds.*

That other shirt, I'm gonna get rid of it. It's scratchy. Do you want it, Xan?

> XAN *shakes her head.*

I guess it's not really your style, is it? Maybe Abby would want it.
JAMIE: Not if it's scratchy.

> *Another text message.* JAMIE *responds.*

CRYSTAL: No, it's not that scratchy. I just don't want it anymore.

> *She leaves the room and comes back with a shirt.*

Here. If she doesn't like it she can just chuck it out. Skip.

> *She plays a Skip card.* XAN *feels skipped.*

It was an expensive top.

> *Another text message.*

RICO: You're popular, aren't you?
CRYSTAL: Who's that?
JAMIE: No-one.
RICO: It's gotta be Abby.

> JAMIE *glares.*

What?
CRYSTAL: Oh, Jamie. I saw on Facebook that there's gonna be a vigil at the high school for Joanna tomorrow. I thought we could go together and then go out to dinner after.
JAMIE: I'm driving back tonight.
CRYSTAL: Well, maybe I'll go.
JAMIE: Why would you go?
CRYSTAL: Because it's nice.
RICO: I'll go with you.
CRYSTAL: We have to wear green.
RICO: No, you wear black. You wear black to a vigil.
CRYSTAL: No, green was her favourite colour. Everyone is wearing green.

> JAMIE *draws a card. He draws another card. He draws about seven cards.*

RICO: Wait, wait, leave some for us!

JAMIE: These aren't the correct rules.

He's still drawing.

RICO: Your arm is gonna get tired!

JAMIE: You realise this game is entirely based on luck. I think I've seen a YouTube clip of a gorilla playing Uno.

He draws more cards.

There's literally no skill involved.

RICO: There's a little skill.

JAMIE: A tiny bit.

RICO: Yeah, yeah. It's minimal. Like five per cent.

JAMIE: I just don't really like this game, there's no strategy.

CRYSTAL: Jamie hates losing.

JAMIE: Oh, do I? Do I hate losing?!

RICO: Whoa! Calm down.

JAMIE: Now you're a psychologist?

CRYSTAL: I'm just your mum.

JAMIE: Well, it's not about losing. I just don't like playing games that are for small children.

He draws a playable card.

There we go. Your fucking turn.

Draw two.

CRYSTAL: I will not. Because. Draw two.

CRYSTAL plays a Draw Two on top of JAMIE's Draw Two. Everyone looks at XAN. XAN does nothing.

XAN: Stop looking at me!

JAMIE: It's your go.

XAN: Oh.

XAN plays a card.

RICO: No. You can't play that. You have to draw four.

XAN: I don't want to play this.

CRYSTAL: What are you talking about? You bought it.

XAN: Stop staring at me. Fuck.

RICO: She's swearing.

CRYSTAL: Are you mad or something?

XAN: Why do you keep asking me that?

CRYSTAL: 'Cause you seem mad.

XAN: I'm not mad.

CRYSTAL: You're just being really quiet.

XAN: Sorry.

Stop looking at me.

Stop looking at me.

JAMIE: Okay. Sorry.

CRYSTAL: What are you sorry about?

JAMIE: I'm sorry for looking at Xan.

CRYSTAL: That's ridiculous. She's just being mopey.

RICO: Why are you being mopey, Xan?

Silence.

CRYSTAL: Are you gonna draw four or not?

RICO: Do you have a Draw Two? You can play a Draw Two. Any colour.

XAN *stands up.*

CRYSTAL: What are you doing?

JAMIE: I think she wants to stop playing.

RICO: Don't be a quitter, Xan!

CRYSTAL: What's that look?

Pause.

RICO: Are you gonna break more dishes?

XAN *looks around. There is a plastic cup on the table. She grabs it and throws it to the ground. It doesn't break. It's plastic.*

CRYSTAL: Are you serious?

XAN *steps on it. It still doesn't break.*

JAMIE: It's plastic.

CRYSTAL: We all know what's it's like to be seventeen, Xan. And you'll live. You'll make it through.

XAN: I don't want to play anymore.

RICO: That's okay. That's fine, man.

XAN *walks to the window and presses herself against the glass. She traces something on the window with her finger, but we can't tell what.*

FANTASY:

The game and conversation continues, but music swells and we can no longer hear anything. XAN *turns and watches her family playing the game. She pushes over a chair. No-one notices. She throws a couch cushion. No-one notices. She rips through the wallpaper on the back wall. Nothing. She bashes a giant hole in the wall. Behind it is a desert and beyond it, an overpass. She steps through the hole.*

Sounds of traffic. The letters 'XOXO' appear on the glass where XAN *was standing earlier.* XAN *climbs to the top of the overpass. She looks out.*

FANTASY ENDS.

5:28PM

RICO *is outside again.* CRYSTAL *sticks her head out the door.*

CRYSTAL: What are you doing out here?
RICO: No.
CRYSTAL: What?
RICO: I mean nothing.

    Pause.

  Is everything okay?
CRYSTAL: Of course. What do you mean?
RICO: Nothing. I don't know.
CRYSTAL: Why are you sitting next to the garbage bin? There's pizza.
RICO: No, I'm just … thinking.
CRYSTAL: Okay.

    Pause.

  About what?
RICO: I don't know.
CRYSTAL: What?
RICO: Just everything. Of people dying mostly.
CRYSTAL: You're thinking about people dying?
RICO: Yeah.
CRYSTAL: Who?

RICO: Just. Um. You. Or Xan. Or me. Or, you know. Any of us.

CRYSTAL: Right. Well.

RICO: Sometimes … sometimes at night I just can't get to sleep because I start thinking about dying, about what it would be like to die, and I just lay there thinking about it and sometimes I … cry.

CRYSTAL: Okay.

RICO: In bed …

CRYSTAL: Okay.

RICO: While you're sleeping …

CRYSTAL: Babe.

RICO: Yeah?

CRYSTAL: It's okay.

A pause. He looks at her strangely.

RICO: Have you gotten some sun?

CRYSTAL: No. What do you mean?

RICO: You know. Some sun.

CRYSTAL: No.

RICO: Well. You look good.

CRYSTAL: Come inside. There's pizza.

Blackout.

5:53 PM

XAN *on the overpass.*

XAN: I'm going to tell you a story.
    It's not about you.
    It's for you.

    So there's this family having dinner in a shitty house. And one of them is Xan. And she gets some bad news. And she finishes her chicken because she has to. And she tries to sleep but she can't. And the next morning she wakes up. Sort of. I mean she hasn't really been asleep so she can't really wake up. I guess what I mean is the next day the sun rises. Somehow. It was pretty unexpected.
    She eats Pringles for breakfast.
    Her mother tells her to clean up the kitchen.
    She doesn't.

She thinks, 'Maybe I should do something, something real, something creative, something for myself'. So she writes a story but it's boring. It's a boring story about this dumb kid that just sits around the house not doing anything, so Xan rips it up and throws it in the bin. (Metaphorically.) (Because I was writing it in my head.) (There wasn't any paper.)

And so she just watches TV.

She watches 'Antiques Roadshow' which usually she finds really calming but today it's just alarming. Desperate people with old, old things that once belonged to other people who are now dead. And the ancestors of the dead people are waving the things in front of a woman asking how much this clock is worth and they don't even remember the person who picked it out, who bought it, who originally touched the thing, maybe saw it in a store and said something like, 'Oh, that's nice, I'd like to have that', and took it home and arranged it on a shelf.

So Xan changes the channel. She watches half an episode of 'Project Runway' and four episodes of 'Gilmore Girls'.

Later the family plays Uno together. It's not a fun game and no-one enjoys it.

A painful shift.

I traced your name on the table.

I decided to stop thinking about you.

I couldn't breathe. Actually couldn't breathe. That's not poetry. That's a panic attack.

I had a moment when everything got fuzzy and tingly and I thought I might shit my pants and I actually sort of enjoyed that feeling except then everyone was staring at me and the feeling turned into my heart beating a little too fast and a weight on my chest and I thought I might faint and my family were like, 'That's a bit of an overreaction to being terrible at Uno', and I thought, 'You're right, it's a bit much, I should leave, I should get out of here', so I did.

And in this story I turn thirty-five or something. And I get promoted to manager of Target. And I'm happy about it. And I marry some dude that is fine. And I have a kid that is okay. And the sun still sets in the west. And the light pisses all over everything and makes you think it's pretty even though it's not. It's still the same as it was when you were alive except now there's a Boost Juice downtown. Maybe I am actually holding a Boost Juice in this story. And I am watching 'The Voice' on TV while I drink it. And I am eating a duck curry. We order Thai food a lot, my family. And we watch 'The Voice' every week. And in summer we holiday on the coast with my parents who pay for the beach house which is nice of them. And we play Uno. And it's boring. And then we all die. One by one. Because everyone dies eventually.

A moment. She takes her mobile phone out of her pocket and dials.

Can you come get me?

6:29 PM

Sound of a vacuum cleaner in the kitchen. The television is on. RICO *is sitting eating pizza, not really watching.* CRYSTAL *enters with a box of broken glass and the vacuum cleaner. She sits.*

CRYSTAL: We're gonna wanna wear shoes in there for a while, I think.

> XAN *and* JAMIE *enter through the front door. No-one knows what to say.*

We got Mario's.

> *Pause.*

RICO: Wanna watch tellie?

> XAN *sits down. They stare at the television.*

XAN: Not this.

> RICO *changes the channel.* XAN *rests her head on* CRYSTAL'*s shoulder.*
>
> *The sound of some dumb show.*
>
> *Blackout.*

THE END

www.ingramcontent.com/pod-product-compliance
Lightning Source LLC
Chambersburg PA
CBHW050022090426
42734CB00021B/3384